Repairing the Damage

Hurricanes
and
Storms

Meldrum Academy

REPAIRING THE DAMAGE

Hurricanes *and* Storms

Clint Twist

EVANS BROTHERS LIMITED

Evans Brothers Limited
2A Portman Mansions
Chiltern Street
London W1M 1LE

© Evans Brothers Limited 1997

First published 1992
Reprinted 1993
First published in paperback 1997
Reprinted 2000

Typeset by Fleetlines Typesetters, Southend-on-Sea
Printed in Spain by GRAFO, S.A. – Bilbao

ISBN 0 237 51799 X

British Library Cataloguing in Publication Data

Twist, Clint
    Hurricanes and storms. – (Repairing the damage)
    1. Hurricanes – Juvenile literature 2. Storms – Juvenile
    literature 3. Natural disasters – Juvenile literature
    I. Title
    363.3'4922

Acknowledgements

Editor: Su Swallow
Design: Neil Sayer
Production: Jenny Mulvanny

Maps: Hardlines, Charlbury
Illustrations: Andrew Calvert

For permission to reproduce copyright material the author and
publishers gratefully acknowledge the following:

Cover (Thunderstorm, Kenya) Gunter Ziesler, Bruce Coleman
Limited
Title page (Lightning, Arizona) Keith Kent, Science Photo
Library **p4** Omikron, Science Photo Library **p5** W Broadhurst,
FLPA **p6** Steve McCutcheon, FLPA **p7** D Nicholls/ECOSCENE **p8**
(top) Hasler and Pierce, NASA GSFC/Science Photo Library,
(inset) NOAA/Science Photo Library, (bottom) Frank W Lane,
FLPA; **p10** (top) Howard Bluestein, Science Photo Library,
(middle) R Steinau, FLPA, (bottom) M J Coe, Oxford Scientific
Films; **p11** Erwin and Peggy Bauer, Bruce Coleman Limited **p12**
Tom Van Sant/GeoSphere Project, Santa Monica/Science
Photo Library **p15** Keith Kent, Science Photo Library **p16** Fritz
Pölking, FLPA **p17** Hoflinger, FLPA **p18** Barnaby's Picture
Library **p19** Australia Information Service, FLPA **p20** Popperfoto
p21 (left) British Red Cross, (top right) Popperfoto/AFP,
(bottom right) Gerald Cubitt, Bruce Coleman Limited **p22**
James Stevenson, Science Photo Library **p23** Mary Evans Picture
Library **p24** Dr Fred Espenak, Science Photo Library **p26** three
eyewitness accounts taken from an article in The Times 16.9.88
by Alan Tomlinson, © Times Newspapers Ltd 1988 **p27**
Bernard Bidault, GAMMA/Frank Spooner Pictures **p28**
S Jonasson, FLPA **p29** David Parker, Science Photo Library **p31**
(top) Cooper/ECOSCENE, (bottom) Ben Fawcett, Oxfam **p33**
(top) D Hoadley, FLPA, (bottom) Harry Nor-Hansen, Science
Photo Library **p35** Dr Jeremy Burgess, Science Photo Library
(inset) Crown copyright **p36** Crown copyright **p37** European
Space Agency/ESA/Science Photo Library, (inset) Dr P Menzel,
Science Photo Library **p38** (left) Robert A Lubeck, Oxford
Scientific Films, (right) National Centre for Atmospheric
Research/Science Photo Library **p39** Vintage Magazine
Company **p40/41** Norm Thomas, Science Photo Library **p42** Dr
Bernard Stonehouse **p43** Mary Evans Picture Library.

The Crown copyright pictures on pages 35 and 36 are
reproduced with the permission of the Controller of HMSO.

The author and publishers have been unable to trace the origin
of the quotations on pages 17, 20 and 36 in order to
acknowledge them.

CONTENTS

INTRODUCTION

Sometimes Nature is far from kind. Sometimes, the very air that we breathe moves with irresistible force, blowing away buildings, trees, and people. We call these displays of elemental power storms. This term covers a wide range of atmospheric events, from small thunderstorms to gigantic storms that cover half an ocean.

Even a small thunderstorm contains a tremendous amount of energy. Only a small part of the total energy is discharged as high-voltage lightning bolts that can split a tree in two. In some countries, thunderstorms often produce tornadoes – thin twisting funnels of wind that suck everything in their path up into the sky. Tornadoes are a very real threat over large areas of the planet's surface.

A hurricane is a hundred times bigger, and thousands of times more powerful, than a thunderstorm. Hurricanes produce the strongest winds on Earth – howling, tearing winds that can strip a town from the land, leaving nothing but a few shattered ruins.

The balance of Nature

We tend to consider storms as unnatural events, disturbances of the balance of Nature. But in fact, storms are a vital part of the process by which the atmosphere makes the surface of our planet habitable. There are very few parts of the Earth's surface that are completely free from the

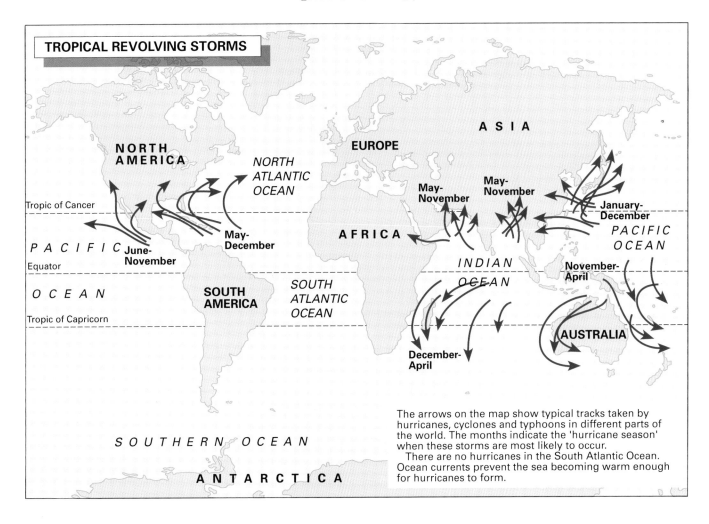

TROPICAL REVOLVING STORMS

The arrows on the map show typical tracks taken by hurricanes, cyclones and typhoons in different parts of the world. The months indicate the 'hurricane season' when these storms are most likely to occur.
There are no hurricanes in the South Atlantic Ocean. Ocean currents prevent the sea becoming warm enough for hurricanes to form.

Hurricanes (left: Palm Beach, Florida, USA in 1949) form out at sea so coastal areas may be exposed to the full fury of the storm.

Crops can be flattened in minutes by storm winds and rain.

threat of storms. Even the driest deserts, and the coldest polar regions, have their own particular types of storm. In the more fortunate areas, truly destructive storms are comparatively rare, occurring only a few times in a century. Elsewhere, however, the storm season is an annual event, and local people have to be on the alert for the first signs of a spinning tropical fury.

During the last 100 years, we have developed the technology that today enables us to keep a constant watch from Space. Every day, photographs from orbiting satellites are studied for the first tell-tale signs of a tropical storm. Advance warning is now possible, but developing nations often lack the resources to evacuate people from the storm's path.

Our scientific success has even tempted us to try to achieve one of our oldest dreams: control over the elements. Despite attempts to tame hurricanes by flying through the teeth of the wind and strewing chemicals, Nature remains unbeaten, and storm winds will continue to blow across the face of the Earth, causing chaos and catastrophe.

CHAPTER ONE

NATURE'S FURY

Thunder clouds

Most people have experienced a thunderstorm: a spectacular display of natural power with strong winds, driving rain and hailstones, the crash of thunder and jagged bolts of lightning. A small thunderstorm covers about 10 square kilometres; a large storm can affect an area some ten times bigger.

A thunderstorm occurs within and beneath a massive cloud formation known as cumulonimbus. Such clouds are often referred to as thunder clouds, or anvil clouds because of their shape. The base of a cumulonimbus cloud is flat and dark grey, and lies between 500 metres and 1500 metres above the Earth's surface. Rising up from the flat base, the cloud is lighter in colour and may tower more than 15 kilometres up into the air (see below).

Although thunderstorms contain great power, about the same as two atomic bombs, they are not particularly destructive. Thunderstorms are part of the normal pattern of weather in many parts of the world. Plants, animals, and buildings are all designed to be able to withstand all but the worst effects of thunderstorms. Inevitably, however, there is some damage. The two most destructive elements of a thunderstorm are hailstones and lightning.

Inside the towering thunder cloud, hailstones can build up to an impressive size. The largest hailstones can weigh up to half a kilogram. This is heavy enough to damage houses and cars, and

Although the storm itself is out of sight behind the trees, the anvil-shaped cumulonimbus cloud can be seen from afar.

Fire started by lightning helps the Banksia, a tropical bush common in Australia, to grow. The flower (left) produces seed pods (top right), which protect the seeds. After a fire has passed, the scorched pods release the seeds, which take root in the newly-cleared ground (above).

to cause serious injury to human beings. Fortunately, hailstones of this size are quite rare, and most weigh only a gramme or two. Natural vegetation may be bruised and bent by hailstones, but it is not usually destroyed by them. Cultivated crops are another matter. Many crops, especially essential food crops such as wheat and maize, are very vulnerable to hailstones. A sudden storm can flatten field upon field of standing crops.

Fire from the sky

A lightning bolt contains tremendous energy, and can blast a 30-metre oak tree into fragments. But blast damage is only a small part of lightning's destructive power. A much greater danger is the threat of fire. Each year, thousands of square kilometres of forests are destroyed by fires started by lightning. However, this too is part of a natural pattern, and most areas will regrow within 50 years. In some parts of the world, the annual burning of vegetation by lightning has become incorporated into the life cycle of several plants.

Lightning can also kill. Each year about 100 people around the world die as a result of being struck by lightning.

Hurricane force

A hurricane is a much bigger storm than a thunderstorm. A hurricane is a huge spinning storm measuring up to 300 kilometres across. At the centre of this raging storm is a calm eye, an area of mild weather and light winds about 15 to 25 kilometres across. Within the rest of the hurricane, screaming winds blow at up to 320kph, carrying great sheets of rain from the cloud wall. Few people have experienced the full effects of a hurricane and survived to tell the tale. A hurricane can wipe out a city, or devastate a small country. There is no foolproof shelter against a hurricane.

Pictures cannot convey what a hurricane feels like, when the air moves over the Earth's surface at more than 200kph. At that speed, a piece of straw can be driven through a wooden plank. Buildings and entire streets are literally torn apart by the tremendous forces and pressures produced by hurricane winds.

The word hurricane is often misused. A hurricane is a tropical revolving storm. Hurricane is the name given to these storms when they occur in the Atlantic Ocean. In the Pacific Ocean they are known as typhoons, and in the Indian Ocean they are called cyclones.

A tropical revolving storm is exactly that. It develops over the sea in the tropics, and revolves very quickly. Very simply, the storm consists of air spiralling upwards. The high wind speeds are caused by air being pulled inwards towards the spiralling updraught. In addition, the whole storm travels at up to 25kph in great sweeping tracks across the globe. Near the centre of the storm, where the wind speed is greatest, this can produce gusts of up to 350kph.

A weather satellite image of the Earth (inset) shows the spiral cloud of Hurricane Allen over the Gulf of Mexico (and a smaller one off the Mexican coast). A magnified image of Hurricane Allen (above) clearly shows the 'eye' of the storm.

An anemometer measures wind speed.

Killers from the sea

The areas most vulnerable to hurricanes are tropical islands and coastlines. Each year a total of about 90 of these storms develop, and although most rage harmlessly out at sea, inevitably some reach land. One of the worst years on record for hurricanes was 1780. In that year, no less than eight separate storms raged through the islands in the Caribbean Sea. The hurricane that struck Jamaica on 3 October 1780 almost wiped out the town of Savannah-la-Mar on the southern coast. An eyewitness account of the scene appeared in a Jamaican newspaper:

'The sea during the last period exhibited a most awful scene; the waves swelled to an amazing height, rushed with an impetuosity not to be described on the land, and in a few minutes determined the fate of all the houses in the bay.
Those whose strength or presence of mind enabled them to seek safety, took refuge in the miserable remains of the habitations, most of which were blown down, or so damaged by the storm, as to be hardly capable of affording a comfortable shelter to the miserable sufferers.
The morning ushered in a scene too shocking for description – bodies of the dead and dying scattered about the watery plains where the town stood . . . The number who have perished is not yet precisely ascertained, but it is imagined some 200 people are lost.'

Storm giants

Terrible though hurricanes and their kind are, they are not the most powerful storms on Earth. That title is reserved for the giant mid-latitude storms that occur in the middle of the Atlantic and Pacific Oceans. These can reach over 3000km across. Because of their immense size, no person or group of people can possibly experience the whole of one of these storms, they are just too big.

Like hurricanes, these mid-latitude storms

Beaufort Scale

Wind speed is often measured according to the internationally-recognised Beaufort Scale. On the Beaufort Scale, force 12 is described as hurricane force. This indicates a wind speed of at least 117kph. It does not mean that the wind was produced by a hurricane.

Force	Approx. speed (kph)	Effects
1	4	smoke drifts
2	10	leaves rustle
3	17	twigs move
4	26	small branches move
5	36	small trees sway
6	48	large branches move
7	58	whole trees move
8	72	small branches break
9	85	houses damaged slightly
10	98	trees broken
11	112	widespread damage
12	117+	violence and destruction

revolve, but they spin much more slowly and over a much greater area. Wind speed never reaches the intensity that it does in a hurricane, but these storms have tremendous influence. Their effects can be observed in the pattern of weather over much of the planet's surface (see Chapter Four).

Whirlwinds

The fastest winds on Earth are those produced by a tornado (or 'twister') – a high-speed suction tube that reaches down out of the sky to wreak havoc. A tornado represents wind in its most concentrated form. Although a tornado is tiny in comparison with other storms, measuring between 10 and 400 metres in diameter, the winds inside a tornado can reach 500kph. In the United States, a tornado once lifted a 350-tonne railway train completely off the tracks, and deposited it about 50 metres away. When a tornado hits a town or village, the results can be devastating.

A tornado funnel (above) is darkened by the soil it has pulled up. Houses in a tornado's path (below) may be shattered while those nearby remain untouched.

Tornadoes occur all over the world, although they are fairly rare in India and Africa. Some countries have more than others. Italy has about ten per year, while England has as many as 60. European tornadoes are quite small and do not cause much damage, and as a result, they are not usually reported. The country with the most, and the most destructive tornadoes is the United States of America.

One region of the southern American plains, stretching from Texas to Missouri, is known as Tornado Alley. Each year more than 300 torna-

does occur within this 600km strip of land. For the local inhabitants, the sudden appearance of a towering, whirling tornado, is almost a weekly occurrence at certain times of year.

Tornadoes have the same basic structure as a hurricane, that of an inwardly-flowing spiral of air. Compared to a 300km-wide hurricane, a tornado is just a spinning thread of air. But because a tornado has a much smaller diameter, it can spin faster. Hence the incredibly high wind speeds and their capacity for destruction. Fortunately, tornadoes are very short-lived events. The average duration is only about 15 minutes, although some last for several hours.

In a tornado, air starts rotating hundreds of metres up in the air. Only when the tornado is fully formed does it reach down to the ground as a thin white tube. The white colour is soon lost as the tornado sucks up soil and dust, and turns a dark grey.

Sand and snow

Hurricanes, thunderstorms and tornadoes all cause damage and loss of life through their sheer speed and power. Other types of storm are dangerous not because of the speed of the wind, but because of what it carries. Light winds are sometimes as dangerous as strong winds. Two substances in particular, sand and snow, create great problems when they are swept up by wind.

Sandstorms, often called dust storms in the United States, occur in all of the world's desert

A sandstorm obscures a village in the Indian Desert.

and semi-desert regions. There are two basic types. The largest is a full-blown sandstorm or khamsin. This occurs when a strong steady wind passes over an area of dry sand or dust, and lifts it into the air. The height to which the sand is carried depends on the wind speed. But even moderate winds of about 20kph can lift sand 200 metres up in the air. In the Sahara Desert, these sandstorms are usually associated with strong seasonal winds that blow from the south. A large sandstorm can blow for days, blotting out the sun over more than 200 square kilometres, swamping roads and smothering fields. In exceptional circumstances, desert dust and sand can be lifted high into the air and carried for thousands of kilometres. In northern Europe, the summer rain is sometimes stained red with dust from the Sahara Desert.

The haboob is a much smaller sandstorm which lasts for only a few hours. A haboob is usually observed in front of an approaching thunderstorm. The sand and dust are blown up into the air by winds blowing out from the storm, and may rise up to 2000 metres. After the thunderstorm has spent its fury, the sand and dust drift back to the surface.

A blizzard is a wind that is laden with snow. Under normal circumstances, snow crystals float gently down from the sky, and everything beneath – ground, trees, houses and cars – gets covered with an even layer of snow. The presence of wind, even light winds, can change this picture dramatically.

When wind is involved, the snow no longer arrives vertically, but at an angle, and it builds up into uneven layers. Areas that are exposed to the wind receive greater amounts of snow, while sheltered areas may get very little. The situation is made even worse when the wind drives fallen snow along the ground, piling it up in great snow drifts.

In January 1977, a 110kph blizzard struck the American city of Buffalo and raged for three days. On average only about 30cm of snow fell during the blizzard, but in some places it had drifted more than 10 metres deep. Nine people froze to death in their cars during this storm.

A strong wind can turn fallen snow into a blizzard (below, in Alberta, Canada).

CHAPTER TWO

WINDS WITHIN A SYSTEM

Temperature control

Our planet is surrounded by an atmosphere, a layer of air that extends 60 kilometres or more above the surface of the Earth. Air consists mainly of a mixture of the gases oxygen, nitrogen, and carbon dioxide, together with small amounts of water vapour.

The atmosphere is our planet's life-support system; it is the oxygen contained in air that allows us to breathe. However, the atmosphere has a much wider role to play than merely the supply of oxygen. The atmosphere shields the Earth's surface from the effects of sunlight. Only a small fraction of the sunlight arriving at the outside of the atmosphere actually reaches the

A view of our planet created by computer from thousands of satellite images. Normally the view is at least partly obscured by clouds in the atmosphere.

surface. The rest of the Sun's energy, in the form of heat, is either reflected or absorbed by the atmosphere. In some ways, the atmosphere acts like a huge heat pump, a machine for moving heat. Heat, caused by sunlight falling on the Earth's surface, is lifted up into the atmosphere where it is lost back into Space.

Heat and pressure

The atmosphere is not a simple, uniform layer of air. High in the atmosphere the air is very thin and individual gas molecules are quite far apart. Close to the Earth's surface the air is much thicker, and the gas molecules are packed fairly close together. The weight of the air above them keeps the molecules tightly packed, and produces what is known as atmospheric pressure. When air is heated, the molecules gain energy and tend to move further apart. If air is heated inside a closed container, the air pressure inside the container will increase as the molecules try to move apart. When air is heated in an open container, for example in the atmosphere, the molecules move apart, and this causes the air pressure to decrease.

Although air is heated as sunlight shines through it, heat is transferred most efficiently by contact with the Earth's surface. Not all parts of the planet's surface receive the same amount of heat energy. The tilt of the Earth's axis means that the area around the equator receives abundant sunlight all year round, while the poles receive sunlight for only part of the year.

A section through the atmosphere

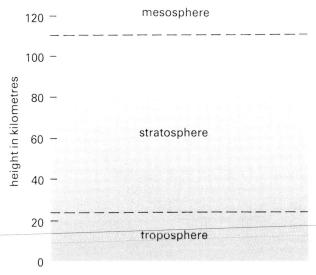

One result of this uneven heating of the Earth's surface is the global wind system. Steady heating around the equator produces a band of permanently low pressure. The air is warmed and rises, carrying heat away from the surface. At the poles, exactly the opposite happens. The intense cold creates areas of permanently high pressure. Although these areas of low and high pressure are far apart, they are connected by the air in the atmosphere. These differences in atmospheric pressure cause the air movement that we call wind.

It is one of the basic principles of Nature that in a fluid (such as water or air) the pressure will be constant at a given depth. If an area of low pressure is created, fluid will tend to move into the low pressure area until the pressure is equalised. At the equator, the Sun's rays create an area of low pressure just above the Earth's surface, which causes air to flow in from the middle latitudes. This air is replaced by cold, high-pressure air from the poles.

Prevailing winds

In simplified form, the basic pattern of air circulation on Earth is that cold air flows downwards from the poles towards the equator, where it is warmed and rises. For the first few kilometres, the temperature drops about 1°C for every 100 metres away from the surface. When the air has cooled, it is pushed back to the poles by the constant updraught from the equator. Over the poles, the air sinks back to Earth to continue the cycle.

This circulation system is known as an atmospheric cell. Earth's atmosphere consists of two such cells, each extending from a pole to the equator. The constant circulation of air through these atmospheric cells produces strong steady air movements at ground level that are known as prevailing winds. In theory, there should be only two prevailing winds, both blowing straight towards the equator. However, this does not take account of the Earth's high-speed rotation.

Our planet and its atmosphere are spinning through Space at a speed of over 1000kph at the equator. This rotation produces Coriolis force, which makes anything that moves freely across

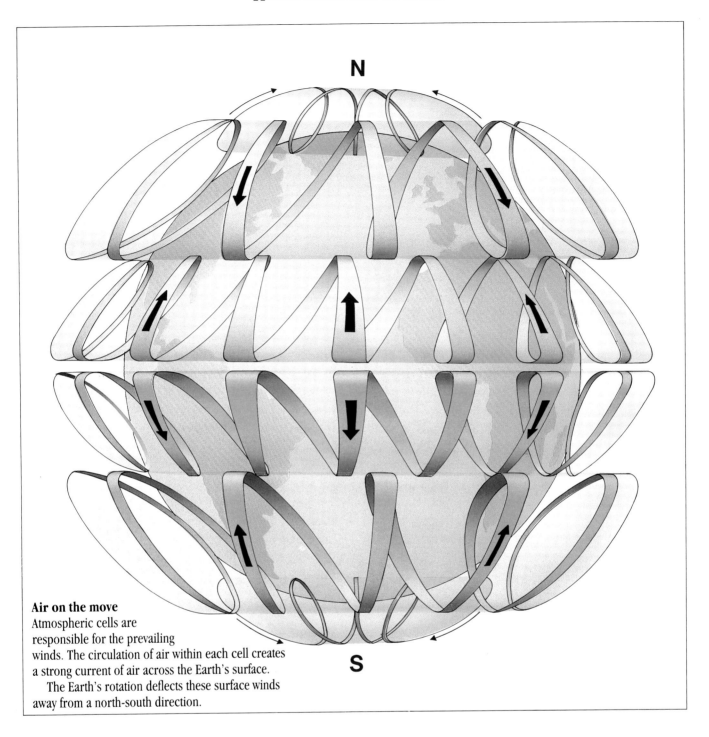

Air on the move
Atmospheric cells are
responsible for the prevailing
winds. The circulation of air within each cell creates
a strong current of air across the Earth's surface.
    The Earth's rotation deflects these surface winds
away from a north-south direction.

the globe follow a slighly curved path. In the
northern hemisphere objects curve to their
right; in the southern hemisphere they curve to
their left. Coriolis force has several important
effects on the circulation of air in the atmosphere. The main effect is to deflect the wind
away from the theoretical north-south path, so
that they blow more or less parallel to the
equator. As a result, the two basic atmospheric
cells break up, so that each hemisphere has
three separate circulation cells. This arrange-
ment produces a series of wind belts that blow
in opposing directions.

Water on the move

So far we have considered the air in the
atmosphere as a single substance. But in terms
of the atmosphere's action as a heat pump, one
particular component of air – water vapour – is
by far the most important. Some of the water
vapour in air is produced by the breathing of
animals and plants, but most is the result of
evaporation from open water surfaces, especially the seas and oceans. At the surface, water
molecules absorb heat energy from sunlight

until they have enough energy to break away from the liquid and become individual molecules of water vapour. The water vapour then mixes with the warm rising air and is carried up into the atmosphere. As the water vapour rises, it cools until it is cold enough to condense back into droplets of liquid water which form clouds. During condensation the water molecules release most of the heat energy they had absorbed from sunlight.

This exchange of heat between the surface and the atmosphere by means of evaporation and condensation is one of the most important functions of the atmosphere. As well as removing excess heat, the water cycle also produces fresh water from salt water. This fresh water may then be carried by the wind for thousands of kilometres before it falls as rain to be used by plants and animals. At any given time, the atmosphere contains enough fresh water to cover the surface of the Earth to a depth of 2.5cm.

A time-delay photograph has captured a series of lightning flashes above Arizona, USA.

Cloud cover

A thunderstorm starts with warm damp air gently rising. A typical storm occurs when two streams of air meet at a front. The cooler air will remain close to the ground, pushing the warmer air upwards. As the air rises, it cools and water vapour condenses into clouds. The rising warm air creates an updraught which pulls in more warm air. As this condenses, the depth of the cloud increases. Within the storm cloud, powerful updraughts carry water droplets high up into the atmosphere where they freeze into hailstones. The cooled air then falls back to Earth, creating the strong wind that often indicates that a thunderstorm is approaching.

For reasons that are still not fully understood, the base of a thundercloud builds up a negative electrical charge. At the same time, the upper portion of the cloud builds up a positive charge. Eventually, the difference between the two electrical charges is so great that electricity travels from one part of the cloud to the other as lightning (sheet lightning).

In addition, the negative charge at the base of

the cloud creates a positive 'shadow charge' in the ground beneath the cloud. As the charge in the cloud builds up, so does the shadow charge beneath it. In many cases, electricity then travels between the ground and the cloud, producing a jagged bolt of lightning.

Despite appearances, a lightning bolt occurs in two stages. The first stage takes place when a weak electrical impulse, known as the 'step leader', passes from the cloud to the ground. The step leader is invisible to the naked eye, and creates a narrow electrical channel between the cloud and the ground. Electricity from the ground then travels up this channel in a spectacular flash of lightning. The visible glow is caused by the air around the channel being heated almost instantaneously to about 30,000°C (about five times hotter than the surface of the Sun). The air expands violently as it is heated, and produces the rumbling sound called thunder.

Birth of a hurricane

A hurricane starts from nothing – it literally forms out of empty air. The exact mechanism is still a mystery, and is likely to remain so. However, we have learned some of the basic conditions for hurricane formation. Hurricanes occur only where the surface temperature of the sea is higher than 26°C. Furthermore, hurricanes do not form within 700 kilometres north or south of the equator. Nor do they occur at all in the South Atlantic (see map on page 5) because ocean currents keep the sea temperature below 26°C. Apart from that, they can form over any tropical sea or ocean.

A hurricane begins with a small disturbance of the atmosphere near the Earth's surface. For example, a thunderstorm, even a sea bird's wing, disturbs the air and creates an updraught (see box). Warm air rises, and surrounding air

Calculating chaos

For many years scientists were puzzled by their inability to predict the behaviour of hurricanes. Hurricanes might be part of a complicated natural system, but they were still governed by the same laws of science and maths that apply to simple systems, or so it was thought. But even with the best measurements and the fastest computers, scientists could not predict the behaviour of a hurricane for more than a few days. Mathematically speaking, hurricanes didn't add up.

Recently, scientists have discovered that the weather operates according to a new branch of mathematics, often called chaotic mathematics. This branch of maths explains why we cannot predict the weather accurately. The global weather system is just too large and complicated. Normal mathematics, which gives predictable results, cannot deal with weather systems. The weather can only be described mathematically by chaotic maths, which gives unpredictable results.

As a result, we have to accept that it is impossible to explain exactly what causes a particular hurricane. Something makes a slight disturbance in the atmosphere – a butterfly flapping its wings in the jungle, someone clapping, or a sea bird landing on the sea. Any or all of these events could create the initial disturbance that leads to the formation of a hurricane. Of course, it is impossible to back track and find out which small movement was responsible for a hurricane.

A waterspout off the coast of Italy

moves in to take its place, and in turn rises. Slowly the updraught builds in strength, and air is pulled in from an ever-increasing area. Because of Coriolis force, the inflow begins to turn in a spiral, which increases the efficiency of the updraught. The spiral turns faster and faster, and becomes a tropical revolving storm, a hurricane with winds up to 300kph.

Once it has built up speed, a hurricane is self-sustaining and gathers energy from the warm sea surface. The hurricane itself is subject to the large influences of the global wind system, and is carried by the prevailing wind. The storm's own motion also influences its direction: the rotation causes it to turn back on itself, spinning away from the equator. Most tropical revolving storms follow a typically curved track.

If the hurricane leaves the ocean and passes over land, it can no longer gather energy efficiently. Land does not conduct heat as well as water does, and the hurricane loses more energy through friction. As a result, the hurricane rapidly blows itself out and dissipates, leaving nothing behind it but devastation.

Twisting the air

Tornadoes do not form out of thin air. In fact, tornadoes are only created in one particular place – inside a towering thunder cloud. As water condenses inside the thunder cloud, it releases large amounts of heat. This heat causes narrow 'chimneys' to form in the cloud, sweeping air upwards in a tight spiral. A large thunder cloud may contain several of these whirling chimneys of air, all at different stages of development.

Once a chimney is spinning fast enough, the spiral of air dips down so that the lower end touches the ground. For a few minutes the tornado rages over the ground until the chimney becomes clogged with soil and debris. The tornado then fades away.

When a tornado forms over a lake or the sea, it creates a waterspout, a tall, spinning column of water. In general, waterspouts tend to be smaller, shorter-lived, and less destructive than tornadoes over land.

Very few people have looked into the inside of a tornado, and lived to tell the tale. In 1928, an American farmer in Kansas paused at the door of his basement tornado shelter and looked over his shoulder:

'Steadily the tornado came on, the end gradually rising above the ground. I could have stood there only a few seconds but so impressed was I with what was going on that it seemed a long time. At last the great shaggy end of the funnel hung directly overhead. Everything was as still as death. There was a screaming, hissing sound coming directly from the end of the funnel. I looked up and to my astonishment I saw right up into the heart of the tornado. There was a circular opening in the centre of the funnel, about 50 or 100 feet (15–30 metres) in diameter, and extending straight upward for a distance of at least one half mile (800 metres) as best as I could judge. The walls of this opening were of rotating clouds and the whole was made brilliantly visible by constant flashes of lightning which zigzagged from side to side.'

CHAPTER THREE

AFTER THE STORM

Clearing up

When the wind and rain have stopped, the signs of a storm's passing are usually visible on the landscape. Leaves and small branches are strewn all over the ground. Larger branches may hang broken, and bushes may have been blown flat. Streams and rivers, swollen with rainwater, may wash soil and vegetation away from their banks. If the storm has been severe, some trees may even have been blown over and become uprooted. During one exceptional storm in 1987 (see Chapter Four), more than 15 million trees were blown over in England alone.

None of this damages the landscape permanently. Leaves and branches are quickly replaced, streams and rivers change their course, and in time new trees will grow where others fell. The natural landscape is a self-repairing mechanism, but the same is not true of human construction.

Houses are generally vulnerable to the wind. Slates, even the whole roof, may be lifted off. Windows and doors can be blown out, chimneys and walls blown over, and wooden buildings may be blown away completely. However, in temperate climates the greatest danger to human life usually comes not from falling buildings, but from falling trees. A car and its occupants are particularly at risk from the sudden collapse of a roadside tree.

Gale force winds uprooted a tree which crushed this van.

Storm damage

The force of a wind depends on its speed. Whether discussing the efficiency of windmills, or the damage caused by storm winds, wind force follows a simple mathematical rule:

Wind force increases with the square of wind speed.

This means that if the wind speed doubles (×2), then the force of the wind increases by four (2×2) times. If the wind speed trebles (×3), then the force increases by a factor of nine (3×3).

The real meaning of this mathematical rule can be better appreciated if the words 'destructive power' are used instead of 'force'. A 60kph wind carries four times the destructive power of a 30kph wind. A 90kph wind carries nine times the destructive power of the 30kph wind. A 180kph gust of wind (by no means rare in violent storms) carries 36 times more destructive power than the 30kph wind.

'It started to hail. The hail turned to rain. There was some terrific thunder. After about an hour, it stopped raining, I walked down the hill. The street was full of water. By the time I got to my house, I was wading up to my knees. Fortunately I lived on the first floor, my flat was dry. But all the people in the basement and ground floor flats were flooded out. Some friends had over two metres of water in their living room and had to be rescued by boat. Rescued by boat at seven o'clock in the evening in the middle of London! I still can't believe it.'

The extent of the damage caused by a hurricane depends on where the hurricane strikes. If the storm blows on to lightly-populated agricultural land, along the coastline of Central America for example, a few thousand hectares of plantation may be destroyed but in some respects this is less costly than if the hurricane hit a rainforest. On agricultural land, the survivors can replant their crops. In the rainforest, there is no one to help, and it can take over 300 years for an area of rainforest to fully recover from hurricane damage.

Town and country

The aftermath of a storm over an area of populated countryside presents a complex picture of public and private damage. The immediate priority is the conservation of human life. Dangerous structures (buildings or trees) must be made safe or demolished, roads and railways must be cleared, power and other services must be restored and transport organised. At an individual level, roofs must be repaired, chimney pots replaced and any debris cleared up.

In towns and cities, the effects of a storm are usually less noticeable and less widespread. Rows of houses provide an effective barrier against strong winds, and there are fewer trees to be blown down. The taller buildings are designed to withstand even the strongest winds. However, city inhabitants are not immune to all the effects of a storm, and may be taken completely by surprise. An office worker recalls one such storm in London in 1975:

When a hurricane strikes a densely populated area, the effect is devastating. After Cyclone Tracy hit northern Australia on Christmas Day 1974, the city of Darwin (population 50,000) had to be virtually rebuilt. New buildings are on stronger, lower stilts.

Storm that changed the world

The most destructive storm in recorded history, and one of the greatest natural disasters of all time, occurred in November 1970. A cyclone came spinning in from the Indian Ocean and hit the mouth of the River Ganges. More than one million lives were lost, a country was devastated, and a new nation arose from the ruins. In order to fully understand the tragedy, it is necessary to understand how a cyclone (or a hurricane or typhoon) can carry the sea with it.

A tropical revolving storm rotates around the eye, the area of apparent calm directly below the central updraught. This updraught has a suction effect on the surface of the sea, lifting the surface under the eye up to two metres above the surrounding sea. This does not sound much, but it must be remembered that the eye of the storm may be up to 30km in diameter. The amount of water lifted by the storm therefore runs into millions of cubic metres. As the storm travels over the sea, it drags with it this low bulge of water, which is known as the storm surge. When the storm hits land, so does the water.

When the cyclone arrived at the Ganges delta, the storm surge hit the land like a bomb. Whole areas were simply washed clean, of plants, animals and people. A farmer who survived the storm recalls the scene:

'About dawn the water began to go down. I could see bodies, hundreds of them, floating out to sea. At about nine in the morning the water finally went down. My farm looked like a desert. There was nothing left, but my family was all right. Only my aunt had been washed away with most of the old people. They were not strong enough to hold onto the trees.'

At that time, the delta area was politically a part of Pakistan, although it was separated by more than 1000 kilometres of India. The survivors blamed the Pakistan government for not giving them enough assistance following the disaster. Many of them argued that they would be better off as an independent country, completely separate from Pakistan. In 1971 the area formally declared itself independent as the new nation of Bangladesh.

A family leave their flooded home on a makeshift raft, after yet another storm hit Bangladesh, in 1974.

Cyclone shelters (left) and mangrove forests (above) help to protect people in Bangladesh from storm floods. Some survivors of the 1991 cyclone had to rely on food supplies dropped by the air force (top).

Since the 1970 cyclone, sea defences have been improved, and a number of cyclone shelters built in the areas most at risk. In April 1991, another cyclone swept in from the Indian Ocean, and once again Bangladesh was lashed by 200kph winds. On this occasion, however, more people were able to survive the terrible storm by taking refuge in cyclone shelters. The shelters are made of concrete and stand two or three storeys high on thick concrete stilts so that they are not swept away by the storm surge. When no storm threatens, the shelters serve as schools, community centres and even as crop stores.

Such shelters are expensive to build, so there are not enough of them. A cheaper alternative that is useful in some places, in all but the fiercest storm, is to build gently-sloping mounds about seven metres high, on which people and their animals can avoid the floodwaters. A small strong building may be added on the top for further protection.

Mangrove forests that run along the coast also offer some protection by breaking the force of the storm surge. Since 1970 the government of Bangladesh has planted some 25,000 hectares of mangrove trees to improve this natural coastal defence. In some places embankments have been built behind the trees. Embankments do not hold the water back for ever, but they do delay the flood so that people have a chance to take shelter.

CHAPTER FOUR

A NIGHT OF STORM

On the night of 15–16 October 1987, southern England was hit by the worst storm for more than 200 years. For four hours, the country experienced the full force of Nature's fury. Along the coastline of the English Channel, wind speeds reached more than 150kph.

Despite the ferocity of the wind, only 19 people were killed as a direct result of the storm. The main reason for this low death toll was that most people were in bed asleep when the storm hit, and the roads were nearly empty of traffic. Had the storm arrived 12 hours earlier or later, during daylight, the chances are that many more people would have died.

Storm damage to property, however, was tremendous. One in six homes in southern England was damaged, and some seven million people were left without electricity. Even worse, about 15 million trees were blown over. As a result, most of the roads and railways leading into London were blocked, and the next day the city almost came to a standstill.

The storm of October 1987 is often, and incorrectly, described as a hurricane. Although the winds certainly reached hurricane force (more than 117kph), the storm was not in fact a hurricane, which is a tropical storm (see page 8). However, a hurricane was involved.

Shop windows in London were blown in by hurricane force winds.

The storm began as a fairly ordinary storm in the Bay of Biscay, off the coast of France and Spain. Normally, the storm would have raged out at sea, and may not have reached land at all. However, this particular storm received a powerful boost from an unexpected source.

On the other side of the Atlantic Ocean, Hurricane Floyd, which had earlier whirled across the coast of Florida, was beginning to dissipate. Floyd was losing energy rapidly, and much of this energy was channelled into a high altitude airstream moving at over 300kph. This high-speed airstream was travelling like a spear, straight towards the Bay of Biscay. In most cases, the airstream would have been deflected long before it reached Europe. But because of the pattern of weather over the Atlantic Ocean at the time, this did not occur. The spear of 300kph winds travelled all the way to its target.

Atmospheric bomb

The airstream produced by the dying breaths of Hurricane Floyd arrived directly above the storm in the Bay of Biscay. When two separate weather systems become linked in this way, it creates what the weathermen call a bomb. The effects are completely unpredictable. Sometimes, the two systems cancel each other out, but this time exactly the opposite happened. The additional energy from Hurricane Floyd greatly increased the power of the storm, and also caused it to turn northwards towards England.

Before reaching England, the storm first swept over northwestern France, causing damage as far inland as Paris, where a giant tower crane collapsed. The worst effects were concentrated in Normandy and Brittany, where 80,000 hectares of ripe corn were flattened, along with millions of trees. It was on the Brittany coast that the highest wind speed of the entire storm, an astonishing 214kph, was recorded.

The great storm of 1703, off the south coast of England

In the heat of the night

One strange effect of the storm was noticed by many people. Just before the storm struck, the temperature suddenly rose by 10 to 15°C, so that midnight became the warmest part of the day. This was caused by warm air from the Bay of Biscay that was carried ahead of the storm. Temperatures remained unusually high for about six hours.

The great storm also produced some very interesting examples of how high winds operate when they scour the landscape almost bare. On a farm in Kent a double avenue of mature trees stood along the drive at right angles to the direction of the storm winds. All night, the wind howled straight across the tree-lined avenue.

The next morning, the trees on one side of the drive were still standing, while those on the other side had been blown over. The strange thing was that the trees that had fallen were on the more sheltered side of the drive.

One possible explanation is that the soil on one side of the drive was much damper and weaker. But a more likely explanation is that the trees were pulled over by suction. As the wind blew through the nearest trees, the air stream was disrupted as it flowed around them. This disruption of the wind stream probably created spiralling air currents known as turbulence vortices. Like tiny and very short-lived tornadoes, these vortices can produce tremendous suction effects. In the same way, it is often found that tiles have been lifted from the edge of a roof that is facing away from the wind.

In perspective

Terrible though it was, the 1987 storm was not the worst ever to strike England. It is generally reckoned that the great storm of 1703 was even worse. That storm, which lasted for a whole week, was responsible for the deaths of some 8,000 people. Although no scientific measurements were taken during the 1703 storm, most experts are agreed that the high death toll indicates that the earlier storm was more powerful. England was much less densely populated at that time, and in order to cause so many casualties, the winds must have been considerably stronger than in 1987.

CHAPTER FIVE

GILBERT'S STORY

Diary of a tropical storm

Storms are fairly common in the southern Caribbean Sea during the late summer. But in September 1988, Hurricane Gilbert, which was probably the most powerful hurricane for 100 years, took the weather forecasters completely by surprise.

Late-summer storms are a part of the annual pattern of weather in that part of the world. The sea retains its heat, creating updraughts of air which lead to storms. In other years, these storms had gone their separate ways, sometimes causing damage, but nothing out of the ordinary. In 1988, however, the storms did not separate as usual but merged together, giving birth to Hurricane Gilbert. Two weeks later, the authorities in about a dozen countries were counting the terrible cost of this unexpected development.

During its 10-day life span, Gilbert killed at least 400 people, injured thousands, and made homeless hundreds of thousands more. The financial cost of Gilbert, in terms of damage to buildings, crops and other property, was enormous, perhaps running into billions of dollars. For some of the poorer countries, Gilbert was a crippling blow to an already shaky national economy.

A satellite view of Hurricane Gilbert as it reached the Yucatan peninsula on 14 September (see map on page 25).

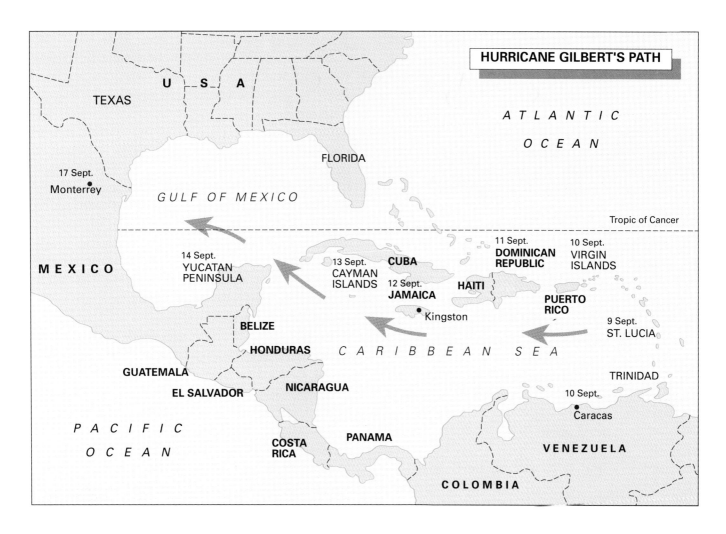

HURRICANE GILBERT'S PATH

The beginning

Friday 9 September – Gilbert had only just emerged as a hurricane-to-be, when it passed over the island of St. Lucia, about 300 kilometres north of Trinidad. The maximum wind speed was only about 50kph (not officially a hurricane). Nevertheless, much of the island's banana crop was destroyed, and most of the tourists left the island immediately, even though none of them had been injured. With a single blow, Gilbert had removed St. Lucia's two most important sources of income. While the islanders started to pick up the pieces, Gilbert moved northwards and eastwards, steadily growing in size and strength.

Saturday 10th – Gilbert was now travelling over an area of open sea; only the northern and southern edges of the storm came into contact with land. But even these glancing blows were enough to cause considerable damage. To the south, Gilbert brushed against Caracas, the capital of Venezuela. In the shanty towns on the outskirts of the city, heavy rains caused several landslides, and at least five people were killed. The northern edge of Gilbert swept through the Virgin Islands, damaging an estimated 10 per cent of houses, and then across the island of Puerto Rico where it caused power cuts in a dozen towns, killed farm animals and destroyed crops.

Sunday 11th – Heat energy absorbed from the sea had caused Gilbert to increase in power. Wind speeds now reached over 120kph and Gilbert was officially declared a hurricane. At sea, 10 fishermen drowned after their boat had been overturned by high winds. On land, Gilbert wreaked havoc across the Dominican Republic and Haiti, killing at least 27 people and leaving thousands homeless.

The middle

Monday 12th – Gilbert changed direction slightly so that the hurricane passed along the whole length of the island of Jamaica At the peak of the storm, winds reached over 225kph, and the results were devastating. Although only about 30 people were killed, over 500,000 (a quarter of the island's population) had their homes destroyed within a few hours. The Prime Minister had no alternative but to declare a national emergency. From above, the capital city Kingston looked like a honeycomb, because almost every house had had its roof blown off. Twisted sheets of corrugated iron roofing lay all over the city, some bent around street lamps like huge bows. Local inhabitants described the devastation:

'Everything in sight is crushed. My wardrobe, my bed, it's all gone. We can't get anything out.'

'I was trembling and crying for mercy and help. The tin roof could have cut off most of our heads.'

'Everything is mashed up and blown away, even my children's clothes are gone. What a sufferation.'

Tuesday 13th – Gilbert swept over the tiny Cayman Islands, causing extensive damage. Out at sea, five Cuban fishing boats with about 80 crew on board were sunk. The wind speed within the hurricane was still increasing steadily.

Wednesday 14th – Gilbert howled across the Yucatan peninsula in southern Mexico. In places, the wind raged at almost 300kph, and thousands of houses had their roofs torn off. Along the coast, there was extensive damage to luxury tourist hotels, and at least 21 people were killed. Gilbert then swept out to sea again, leaving misery and destruction behind.

The end

Thursday 15th – Gilbert was now officially rated a force 5 hurricane, the highest rating for a tropical storm, and there was every indication that Gilbert was heading straight for Texas. The last time a force 5 hurricane had struck the United States (Hurricane Camille in 1969), over

250 people had been killed. This time the authorities were taking no chances. A hurricane warning was issued for the whole stretch of coastline between New Orleans and the border with Mexico.

Friday 16th – Then during the second day of crossing the Gulf of Mexico, Gilbert began to lose energy. Maximum wind speeds dropped back to about 200kph, and Gilbert was down-rated to a force 3 hurricane. This still represented a serious threat, but not the impending disaster that had been feared. Along the southern coast of the United States, the inhabitants prepared for a big blow. Thousands were evacuated, and the Red Cross set up relief centres further inland.

Saturday 17th During the small hours of the morning, and probably because the storm was losing energy, Gilbert swerved inland, crossing the Mexican coast about 200 kilometres south of the United States.

The Mexican authorities had issued no warnings; they believed that Gilbert would pass to the north. Immediately in the hurricane's path was the flourishing fishing village of La Presca. Afterwards, a Mexican official announced, 'La Presca looks as if it has been flattened by a steamroller.' Further south in the town of Tampico, the storm surge raised the sea level by some two metres and caused widespread flooding. Gilbert continued inland, causing the greatest damage at Monterrey, Mexico's third largest city. Although the winds had slowed to about 120kph, Gilbert still carried plenty of rain, and it was this that caused the greatest loss of life. In the city centre, four buses packed with people were swept away by a sudden rush of floodwater that turned a dry river bed into a raging torrent. Six policemen from the city's special rescue squad were drowned while attempting to reach survivors. Of more than 180 people on the four buses, only about a dozen escaped with their lives. The city authorities also reported that 60 people had been killed by landslides and falling buildings.

Sunday 18th – Gilbert eventually entered the United States near the Mexican town of Nuevo Laredo, but by this time the winds were down to about 50kph. Very little damage was caused in the United States, and some 100,000 Americans who had evacuated their homes breathed a huge sigh of relief. But not everyone escaped unharmed. In San Antonio, Texas, about 300km north of Monterrey, a man was killed while he sat in a chair in his front room. High winds snapped a telegraph pole which fell through the window of his house.

When Hurricane Gilbert swept across the Yucatan peninsula, hundreds of thousands of people were left homeless. About 11,000 tourists were evacuated from the coastal resort of Cancun (right and below).

CHAPTER SIX

PROTECTING LIVES AND LAND

Keeping safe

Although it is in itself harmless, the crash of thunder serves as a timely warning that storms can be dangerous. However, compared with a hurricane or a tornado, a thunderstorm presents only a small risk to human life. This risk can be reduced even further by following a few simple, common-sense precautions.

At the approach of a storm, the most important thing is to avoid trees and especially not to seek shelter under a tree. Experience has shown that trees are liable to be blown over by storm winds, particularly if the soil around their roots has been loosened by torrential rain. This advice applies to motorists as well as those on foot. Being in a car tends to give the driver and passengers a false sense of security during a storm. The same vehicle that protects them from the rain can easily turn into a deathtrap if it is hit by a falling tree.

The other reason for avoiding trees during a storm is because they attract lightning. In normal circumstances, lightning will make contact with the nearest electrical conductor. Trees are not good conductors of electricity, but they stand higher than the surrounding ground, and therefore make likely targets. A human being standing in the open can also provide the nearest electrical conductor. If caught in a storm, the safest thing to do is lie on the ground.

Waving a metal object, such as a golf club, in the air during a storm is an extremely foolish thing to do. The metal provides the lightning with a very attractive conductor. On average, at least one golfer is killed by lightning each year.

Buildings and other tall structures are usually protected by a lightning conductor. A metal rod is fixed to the highest point of the roof, and attached to the ground by a strip of copper which runs down the outside of the building. The metal copper is an excellent conductor of electricity. If lightning strikes, the electrical charge is conducted harmlessly down the copper strip to the ground.

Other precautions against storm damage are just plain common sense. Doors and windows should be closed and secured, and if shutters are fitted, they may be fastened across windows. Less obvious is the need for immediate inspection after a storm. Sometimes, storm damage is not readily apparent. Buildings and trees may have been seriously weakened, without actually collapsing. Unless this damage is located and remedied, they may fall with the next strong gust of wind, causing further damage or injury.

Forecasts and warnings

At sea, storms present a much greater threat, especially to small fishing boats and pleasure craft. For this reason, many countries issue special shipping forecasts for their coastal waters. These forecasts are broadcast by radio and are usually prepared daily by the coastguard or similar national authority. The waters around

A lightning conductor (right) in New Mexico is part of an array of instruments at a laboratory which specialises in lightning and atmospheric research. A rocket (inset) is designed to carry a wire into the clouds to attract lightning.

Shipping forecasts are essential for fishermen.

the coast are normally divided into areas about 100 kilometres wide. For each of these a detailed forecast is made, noting the speed and direction of the wind, visibility, and the anticipated state of the sea and height of the waves.

Particular attention is drawn to the development and duration of any storms. If winds above about 65kph (enough to break small branches off trees) are expected, then the authorities will issue an official gale warning. People who spend all their time on land pay little attention to the shipping forecasts. But for sailors, these forecasts are an essential service. Around the world, untold thousands of lives have been saved by gale warnings.

Gale warnings are a routine part of weather forecasting, but a hurricane warning is a full-scale emergency. Once issued, the warning is continually repeated on radio and television so that as many people as possible get the message in time. If you hear a hurricane warning, there is only one sensible course of action – to get out of the way. Coastal districts, towns and cities are often evacuated completely if they lie in the expected path of a hurricane. Some attempt may be made to protect property, for example windows can be boarded up and boats fitted with extra anchors. However, these attempts are usually futile. If the hurricane strikes, boarding and anchors stand little chance against 200kph winds.

If escape is impossible, the best place to be is inside a solidly-constructed building, preferably in the basement or under the stairs. If no suitable shelter is available, lying flat on the ground, ideally in a ditch, means there is less chance of being blown away or hit by flying debris. When the wind dies down, people should stay in their safe places. There will be a lull while the eye of the hurricane passes, then the wind will rapidly speed up again, this time blowing from the opposite direction.

The panic caused by a hurricane warning can be almost as disruptive as the effects of the hurricane itself. For this reason, the warning is usually issued in two stages. A hurricane alert is issued several days beforehand over the entire area threatened by the hurricane. This alert places all the emergency services in a state of maximum readiness. The hurricane warning itself is issued 24 hours before the hurricane

Tempting fate

The worst thing that you can do on hearing a hurricane warning is to hold a hurricane party. These parties became very fashionable during the 1950s among people living on the southeastern coast of the United States. Instead of evacuating when they heard the warning, the inhabitants would invite their friends round to watch the wind and waves. Sometimes these thrill-seekers were lucky, other times they were not. One such party was held at a beach-front house on 17 August 1969. Hurricane Camille was predicted to arrive some 150 kilometres to the east, so the party-goers thought that they were in for a safe show. But Camille suddenly changed direction and arrived directly overhead. The house was demolished, and of 24 party-goers, only one survived to tell the tale.

arrives, when the forecasters have a better idea of where exactly it will strike.

This two-stage method provides the best balance between saving life and keeping disruption to a minimum. The main problem is that the hurricane's track remains unpredictable right up to the last minute. If the warning is issued too soon, then millions of people may be evacuated unnecessarily. If the forecasters wait until they are certain where the hurricane will arrive, then there will not be enough time for people to get out of the way. Even using the most modern techniques (see Chapter Seven) the 24-hour warning may contain an error of up to 150 kilometres in predicting the path the hurricane will follow.

Sea defences

The coastline is the most dangerous place to be during a hurricane or any other storm. Quite apart from being exposed to the full force of the wind, the coast is also vulnerable to the sea itself. Hurricanes are the only storms that actually carry the sea with them (see page 20), but lesser storms can produce waves which wash away beaches and swamp coastal towns.

The simplest form of sea defence is the sea wall, a physical barrier to keep the water out. Sea walls are found along many coastlines, especially those that experience frequent storms. On some walls, the side facing the sea is curved so that waves are deflected back out to sea. However, these traditional solid walls are very expensive to build and maintain. Recently, engineers have developed cheaper methods of sea defence. These may look less impressive than a solid wall, but they can be more effective.

As well as providing a physical barrier against salt water, sea defences must also absorb the energy contained in storm waves. A solid wall is not the best method of doing this. Some sea defences now incorporate a pile of concrete blocks in front of the sea wall. The blocks are piled up in jumbled heaps, the more loosely the better because it is the gaps in between the blocks that absorb most of the energy.

Another method is to coat the face of the sea

In Holland concrete barriers are used to protect low-lying land against flooding.

Villagers in Vietnam build an embankment of mud to protect their land against flooding.

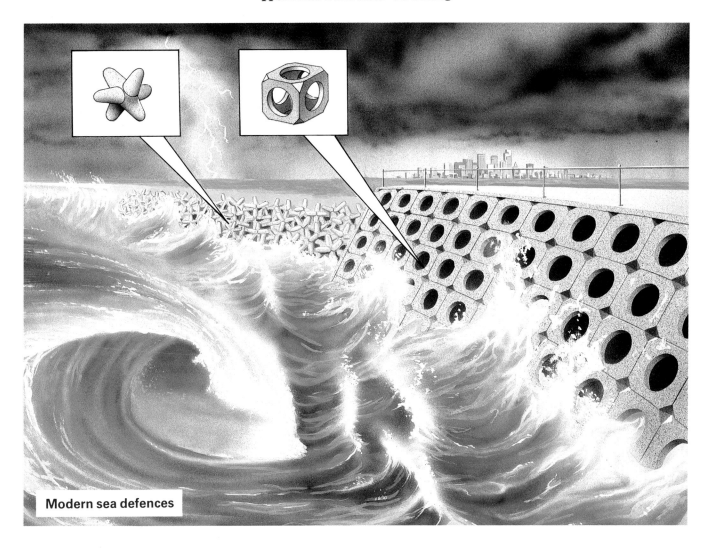

Modern sea defences

wall with a layer of hollow concrete cubes. These measure about a metre across, and have a circular opening in each face. The blocks are fitted very closely together so that they form a honeycomb that completely covers the face of the wall. When a wave strikes the honeycomb, the water rushes into the circular openings, and is swirled round inside the cubes where it loses energy. The other great advantage of the honeycomb method is that it uses only half the amount of concrete used by other barriers, so it is more economic.

Plastic seaweed

Offshore oil and gas platforms are particularly at risk from violent storms. Building a separate sea wall round each platform is obviously out of the question, as many platforms operate in water over 50 metres deep. Moving a platform out of the way of an approaching storm is equally impractical. Locating a platform in the correct position can take several weeks, and moving them is an extremely expensive business. In general, offshore platforms have to be able to withstand the very worst weather conditions.

On top of the platform, equipment can be lashed down and secured against high winds. A much greater threat comes from the rough seas produced by storms. The energy contained in large waves can topple even the most stable and securely anchored platform. One novel defence against the force of the waves is the use of artificial seaweed.

Around some of the platforms in the North Sea, large plastic mats have been anchored to the sea bottom. Attached to these mats are long strands of buoyant plastic which float in an upright position. Although each individual strand presents very little resistance to the wave force, the result of using thousands of such strands is remarkable. The effect is the same as wind blowing through a forest. Most of the energy is absorbed, and very little passes through to the other side.

Tornado approaching

Tornadoes are the most localised and unpredictable of the big winds. A tornado descends from a storm cloud without warning, and rarely lasts for more than an hour. Accurate warnings are impossible in such circumstances, there just isn't enough time. The best that the authorities can do is to alert people on the days that tornadoes are thought most likely to occur. Apart from that, avoiding a tornado is really a matter of keeping your eyes open.

Outdoors, a tornado can be seen and heard up to 30 kilometres away. The important thing is not to panic; observe the tornado's path of travel, then move away at right angles. Tornadoes present a much greater threat to those indoors, who may not hear the twister coming. In America's Tornado Alley, and in other parts of the world where tornadoes are frequent, most buildings have basement tornado shelters. These shelters are the only safe way of remaining in the tornado's path. If there is time, damage to houses can be minimised by taking simple precautions. One of the most destructive aspects of tornadoes is the great difference in air pressure between the centre of the twister and the surrounding atmosphere. This difference in pressure can cause houses to literally burst apart. The chances of this happening are reduced if the doors and windows at the side facing the tornado are securely closed, while those on the opposite side are left open. This allows the air pressure to equalise and prevent the house from 'exploding'.

A tornado shelter in Texas, USA, is set into the ground.

Plastic seaweed (inset) can protect oil rigs from the full force of storm waves.

CHAPTER SEVEN

PREDICTING THE FUTURE

A search for accuracy

Our main defence against hurricanes and other violent storms is timely and accurate weather forecasting. A weather forecast consists of two separate stages. Firstly, the weather signs must be observed and interpreted correctly; and secondly, a prediction based on that interpretation must be communicated to the public.

A weather event, such as a violent storm, cannot be observed until it happens. Experienced observers may be able to identify conditions that make a storm likely, but until a storm develops even the best predictions contain a large element of guesswork. Once a storm has developed, however, it is a different story. As storms and hurricanes travel across the Earth's surface, their progress can be noted and studied, and a much more accurate forecast of their future behaviour can be made.

Communications progress

A hundred years ago, most information travelled very slowly, no faster than a galloping horse. On land, the telephone and telegraph had only just begun to speed up the process of communication. However, their use was restricted to a few large cities. At sea, where the worst weather develops, the situation was even worse. Advance warning of a hurricane depended on an extremely fortunate series of events. Firstly a ship had to survive its encounter. Then it had to sail ahead of the storm, and reach port before the hurricane did. In these circumstances, a hurricane warning service was out of the question. Most hurricanes struck land without any warning at all, and the death toll was much higher than it usually is today. During the last 100 years, a series of technological advances has enabled information to outrun a storm. As a result, the world is now a safer place.

Radio reports at sea

Point-to-point communication without wires (that is, by wireless) was first installed on ships during the early 1900s. As well as allowing ships to warn each other of bad weather, the new radio equipment also enabled weather information to be sent back to land ahead of any storm. For the first time, inhabitants of coastal areas had a real chance of finding out that a hurricane was coming before it hit them. By collecting reports from different ships at different times and places, weather experts could determine the speed and direction of the storm.

Relying on chance encounters with storms was a fairly hit or miss affair, and several countries sent out special weather ships fitted with sensitive equipment for measuring air pressure, wind speed and humidity. Each weather ship patrolled a small sector of the ocean, staying out at sea for months at a time. Correctly positioned, a fleet of weather ships could radio advance warning of bad weather approaching from any direction. Although they may seem somewhat old-fashioned, weather ships are still very important today. They provide accurate measurement of conditions at the sea surface, information which is not otherwise available.

Air patrols

The next great advance in weather forecasting came with the development of the aeroplane. Previously, scientists had been fairly limited in the observations that they could make. Recording instruments could be sent aloft by balloon, but their recovery was a very uncertain affair. For the most part, scientific observation of the weather was limited to the Earth's surface. The

Thick cloud cover can prevent weather satellites from picking up clear information about conditions at sea level, but weather buoys (inset) can be used to collect the data.

ODAS 21 G

power of flight allowed the investigation of a large section of the atmosphere, not just the layer in contact with the surface.

The aeroplane also had other advantages. Flying at 500kph, a single aeroplane could patrol and observe a much greater area of ocean than a weather ship. By the mid-1940s, the US Navy was flying regular air patrols to provide warning of approaching hurricanes. In addition, aeroplanes could also be sent to monitor the progress of a particular storm, and to fly through a hurricane, to find out what really happens.

On 15 September 1945, Lieutenant James P Dalton took off from Florida to investigate a full-strength Atlantic hurricane:

'One minute this plane, seemingly under control, would suddenly wrench itself free, throw itself into a vertical bank and head straight for the steaming white sea below. An instant later it was on the other wing, this time climbing with its nose down at an ungodly speed. I stood on my hands as much as I did on my feet. Rain was so heavy it was as if we were flying through the sea like a submarine. Navigation was practically impossible. For not a minute could we say we were moving in any single direction – at one time I recorded 28 degrees drift, two minutes later it was from the opposite direction almost as strong. At one time our presssure altimeter was indicating 2,600 feet due to the drop in pressure, when we actually were at 700 feet. I don't know how close we came to the sea, but it was far too close to suit my fancy.'

Aeroplanes (below) and meteorological balloons (inset) are used to obtain weather information at relatively low levels in the atmosphere.

Satellites

After having a look from the air, the next step was to take a view of the weather from Space. The first weather satellite, TIROS, was launched in 1960, and within days it had located an unsuspected typhoon in the South Pacific.

One of the first things to be learned from weather satellites, was that hurricanes are more common than was previously thought. About half the hurricanes each year occur harmlessly out of human sight, and are seen only by satellites. In many respects, hurricanes are ideal events for satellite observation. They are large, and produce a characteristic spiralling cloud formation. The eye of the hurricane shows up as a clear spot in the centre of the cloud. As a result, the progress of the storm can be follo-wed with great accuracy from a series of satellite photographs. However, ordinary cameras can only record details at the top of the cloud layer. Events inside the hurricane are obscured by cloud and remain mysterious. Other types of detection devices can provide some of the missing information. Radar waves reflecting off the water droplets can be used to build up a three-dimensional picture of the cloud structure. Heat-sensitive infrared cameras can also map the pattern of heat distribution in the upper layers of cloud. But even with the most sophisticated techniques, satellites cannot tell us everything. A tornado occurs between the bottom of the cloud layer and the planet's surface. From above the cloud layer, there may be no indication that a tornado exists.

The European Remote-sensing Satellite (ERS-1) (an artist's impression, below) is designed to measure winds, ocean currents and long-term climate change.
A heat map (inset) of the atmosphere produced by satellite shows the hottest areas as black, and decreasing temperatures as blue, green and red and the coldest as white.

Hailstones

Layers of ice build up on hailstones (left) as they alternately melt and freeze as they are whirled up and down inside a storm cloud. These layers show up clearly in this cross-section (below) of a large hailstone as big as a grapefruit.

Weather maps

In one respect, weather forecasting has changed little during the last 2000 years – we still watch clouds in order to know what the weather will do next. In Roman times, farmers and sailors anxiously scanned the skies for clouds that meant the approach of bad weather. Today, the cloud formations are photographed from Space and the pictures transmitted back to Earth. Although satellite photographs are useful, they actually provide a very limited amount of information. A much clearer picture of what is happening to the weather is provided by weather maps. These are compiled from hundreds of measurements taken at different weather stations around the country.

The basic shape of the weather is revealed by the isobars – lines that join places with the same atmospheric pressure. Isobars show the location of areas of high and low pressure. From this, the direction of the winds can be deduced, because winds always blow from high to low pressure. The speed of the wind can also be estimated. When the isobars are close together, and there is a steep pressure gradient, then the winds will be strong. When the isobars are spaced widely apart in a gradual pressure gradient, the wind speed will be much less. On some weather maps, the direction of the wind is indicated by arrows with numbers giving the wind speed.

The other main feature of weather maps is the location and extent of fronts. A front is the forward edge of an airstream that is significantly warmer or colder than the surrounding atmosphere. The approach of a warm front usually means that temperatures will rise. A cold front, on the other hand, will cause temperatures to fall. An occluded front occurs when fronts of differing temperatures come into contact with each other. The result is that one front pushes the other higher into the atmosphere. It is the interaction of these various factors – pressure, wind speed, temperature, and the movement of fronts – that provides the fine detail of local weather, rain or shine.

Hurricane off course

Today, satellites provide us with a constant flow of information concerning the weather. As a result, modern weather forecasting is about 85 per cent accurate over a period of 48 hours. Serious mistakes are very rare, and people can be confident that a hurricane will not arrive without warning. In the past, however, weather forecasting was a much less exact science.

By 1938, the United States had developed a fairly comprehensive hurricane forecasting service. A hurricane had struck the coast on average once a year for 10 years, and the authorities thought that they knew what to expect. On 16 September, a hurricane was spotted off the island of Puerto Rico heading for the Florida coast. The forecasters studied the storm's progress, and predicted that the hurricane would strike on 20 September. A warning was issued, and throughout 19 September the inhabitants of Miami and other towns in Florida boarded up windows and moved inland. The next day, nothing happened. The hurricane veered off course.

The authorities were greatly relieved. Experience had shown them that some hurricanes were likely to spin off out to sea without doing any damage. However, they were mistaken, and because all the shipping had moved out of the area in response to the warning, nobody noticed what had really happened until it was too late. Instead of moving out to sea, the hurricane had speeded up and travelled north.

At three o'clock in the afternoon on 21 September, the hurricane hit Long Island, just off the coast next to New York City. During the next seven hours the hurricane travelled 450 kilometres up the valley of the Connecticut River, taking 200kph winds deep inland where they had never been experienced before. The inhabitants were completely unprepared, and within that short space of time, more than 600 people were killed, and many thousands of homes were destroyed.

Trees and telegraph poles were blown over by the 1938 hurricane when it struck Providence, Rhode Island, USA. The damage elsewhere was even more devastating.

CHAPTER EIGHT

CLIMATE CHANGE AND WEATHER CONTROL

Storms and hurricanes are a major component of our planet's climate system. Scientists and weathermen may not be able to forecast exactly when storms will occur, but they can predict the range of likely weather conditions for a particular time and place. They can do this because Earth's climate system is stable, the same sort of conditions occur year after year. However, a stable system does not mean that the weather is always the same.

Away from the equator, the weather is greatly influenced by the annual cycle of the seasons. Hurricanes and tornadoes are most likely to occur during certain months of the year. Beyond this annual cycle, there may be longer cycles. Studies of hurricanes in the Atlantic Ocean seem to indicate that hurricane activity follows an approximate 35-year cycle. The worst hurricane years occur every 30 to 40 years. Other weather cycles are much longer — the climate has not always been as it is today.

About 100,000 years ago, the climate was much colder. At that time, the Earth was in the middle of an ice age. Most of Europe and North America were covered with a year-round layer of ice and snow. Since then, temperatures have got warmer, but the climate has not remained constant. For example, between AD1200 and 1700 average temperatures went down, and this period is often described as a mini ice age. Today, the planet is warming up again.

Global warming

Earlier this century, scientists became aware that our planet was getting warmer. At first they thought that this warming was part of the natural cycle of climate that produced the Ice Age. Recently, however, most scientists have become convinced that the warming is due to the fact that the atmosphere is being changed by air pollution.

Air pollution is normally associated with smoke that produces smogs and acid rain. But in fact the most dangerous form of air pollution is the invisible gas carbon dioxide. This gas is naturally present in the atmosphere, but it is produced in large quantities by burning fuels such as coal, oil and natural gas. Modern civilisation produces so much carbon dioxide that the percentage in the atmosphere is actually increasing.

More carbon dioxide in the atmosphere means that the atmosphere can absorb more of the sun's energy. This extra energy becomes trapped in the atmosphere as heat. As a result,

Some forms of pollution, such as waste heat, are invisible. Waste heat from factories and offices could be adding to global warming.

the average temperature of the air increases. Some scientists have predicted that the average temperature will increase by a further 4°C during the next 40 years. This could have worldwide disastrous effects.

Increased temperatures will mean that large areas of the planet's polar ice caps will melt. The level of the sea could rise between two and eight metres, flooding thousands of square kilometres of coastal land.

The effects of global warming on storms and hurricanes is very hard to predict. Higher temperatures may, for example, cause hurricanes to become even more powerful as they pump heat away from the planet's surface. However, the increased temperatures may also lead to greater evaporation, which means thicker clouds. These clouds may block out sunlight, so that the surface of the sea never gets warm enough to produce the beginnings of a hurricane. One thing is fairly certain: global warming is going to change the pattern of climate on Earth, and a recent series of violent storms has convinced some people that this is already happening.

Global warming would cause ice in the polar regions to melt, and the sea level would rise.

Man-made snow and rain

Control of the weather is one of the oldest human dreams. In many societies, control of the weather was thought to rest with the gods. Attempts at weather control, for instance to bring rain for crops, usually involved great ceremony, with a lot of drums and noise to imitate thunder. Ever since humans learned the scientific basis of weather patterns, they have been trying to use science to control the weather.

Attempts at scientific weather control first began during the 1940s when American scientists were investigating how snow crystals formed in clouds. They believed that the crystals must form round something, and they tried over 100 different substances such as dust and salt. Finally they discovered a substance that produced perfect snow crystals every time – solid carbon dioxide, which is popularly known as dry ice. Although carbon dioxide is normally a gas, it freezes at −40°C. In the laboratory, dry ice produced a scattering of snowflakes from an artificial cloud. When dry ice was scattered from an aeroplane on to a real cloud, it produced nearly 20cm of snow on a November

At the beginning of this century, farmers in France and Italy were developing ways to protect their crops from hailstone damage. This French device was used to fire gunpowder at the clouds and was apparently quite successful at making it rain before hailstones could develop. Today, similar techniques are used to protect crops in, for example, Italy and the USSR.

day that had been forecast as 'fair and warmer'.

Dry ice is fairly inconvenient to handle because it has to be kept at a low temperature, and quite large amounts have to be used. The scientists continued to search for other substances that would provide snow or rain. In 1947, they discovered that a dust made from the chemical silver iodide worked much better than dry ice. Only a few kilograms of silver iodide were needed to produce rain from large clouds.

The technique of scattering dry ice or silver iodide is known as cloud seeding. Usually the task is carried out by specially equipped aeroplanes, but in Italy individual farmers send up thousands of small rockets each year. The Russian government uses cloud-seeding aircraft to protect crops from hailstone damage. Seeding the clouds makes the hailstones fall before they get big enough to cause any harm. In general, however, cloud seeding is not widely employed. The results are by no means certain, and there is considerable concern about the pollution effects of scattering large amounts of chemicals into the air.

Stopping a storm

The most ambitious attempts at weather control have been directed against hurricanes. The apparent success of early cloud-seeding experiments convinced some scientists that they could use the technique to slow down, or even stop a hurricane in its track. They argued that by speeding up the process at which liquid water turned into ice, cloud seeding would cool down the hurricane. In turn this would cause the wind to slow down to less damaging speeds.

The first attempts to prove this theory with dry ice or silver iodide ended in failure, and in 1965 one experiment was blamed for making Hurricane Betsy swerve off course and hit Florida. But in 1969, Project Stormfury had a remarkable success. A series of cloud-seeding flights caused the wind speed inside Hurricane Debbie to drop from 180kph to 125kph, a decrease of 30 per cent.

Although 125kph is still officially a hurricane-force wind, it only causes about half the damage of a 180mph wind. Unfortunately, Project Stormfury was not able to repeat this success with other hurricanes, and large-scale weather control experiments have been halted.

Hurricanes and storms are part of the natural process of life on Earth. In time, natural ecosystems will recover from even the worst storm damage; our planet heals itself. People, on the other hand, are much more vulnerable. In theory, it is possible to protect everybody from the effects of storms. The best buildings can withstand even the worst storms. But life is usually not that simple.

Developing countries often find it difficult to strike the right balance. With only limited resources at their disposal, storm shelters are just one of the many projects demanding their attention. Recent experience has shown that when shelters are provided, they can save lives. But no government can be expected to provide shelters for all of its citizens against all of life's risks.

The facts are quite straightforward — storms are a threat to human activity in all parts of the world. Experience has shown that we cannot control or shape the weather, all we can do is protect as many people as possible, and repair the damage where we can.

GLOSSARY

airstream – a forceful movement of air within the atmosphere; a volume of air having the same temperature and moving in a particular direction.

atmosphere – layer of air 60 to 100km deep that surrounds our planet.

atmospheric cell – pattern of air circulation within the atmosphere.

atmospheric pressure – force exerted in all directions by the weight of air above. Atmospheric pressure is normally measured at sea level.

chaotic mathematics – system of mathematics that follows the irreversible changes of the natural world. Also known as chaos theory.

Coriolis force – force produced by Earth's rotation, that makes objects follow a slightly curved path through the atmosphere.

isobar – line on a weather map that connects points with the same atmospheric pressure.

mid-latitudes – areas of the planet's surface midway between the equator and the poles.

molecule – the simplest unit of a chemical element or compound.

prevailing wind – strong steady wind produced by atmospheric cells and influenced by the Earth's rotation.

step-leader – invisible discharge of electricity that precedes a bolt of lightning.

tornado – narrow column of rapidly rotating air that is produced by a thunderstorm.

tropics – area of the planet's surface between the Tropics of Cancer and Capricorn.

vortex (plural **vortices**) – a spinning current of air caused by the disruption of air flow.

water vapour – water in the form of gas.

INDEX